## Introduction

Hi all. For those of you who don't know me well, I'm Danielle McGaw, The Social Freelance Writer. I've been writing online for more than 7 years and I've been infatuated with social media - mostly Facebook and Twitter, since I discovered them.

I think that social media definitely should play a part in the freelance writer's marketing strategy and I think that it can be a valuable tool for connecting with people that could use your services.

This e-book is filled with some of my best blog posts that were written specifically with freelance writers in mind. I think that there is a lot of information that will be helpful to new freelance writers but even those who have been writing online for awhile might find some of this useful.

And yes, you could just go onto the blog and read the original versions. But then you would miss out on all the **new and updated freelance writing and social media goodness!** I wouldn't just try to sell you stuff you can get on the blog for free! ☺

Each post has been added to and has new information for you to benefit from. Each post has a suggested To Do List that you can use to make your writing or your social media strategy better. **Each post has added value!**

## Why I Quit My Job to Work from Home Full Time

You know, I am sure there are a lot of people who don't understand why I quit my job a year ago so that I could write and work from home full time (BTW, now that I think of it – I just passed my two year anniversary of being a full time work from home mom!  It was June 28th, I think!).

Some people think that it was because I make a lot of money.

**I'm sorry but I don't.**

Some think that it was because I hated my job.

**I didn't.**

Yet others just put this label of **success** on me.

I don't think of myself that way.

I'm just someone that figured out a way to make a living by doing what she loves!

I quit a reliable job with benefits that was reasonably close to home and let me take a day off whenever I needed to be with my kids because I just couldn't see any other life for myself. Working from home and writing are the only things I've ever really wanted to do.

Sure, I went to school and had these ideas of working in social services. I still think I could have been content in a job like that. I was taking Human Ecology with a Family Studies major when I was in University and I loved the things I learned. But the whole time I was in University I was more thrilled about the tiny, low paying writing jobs that I got than I ever was about an A in any course. Except the writing ones. ☺

I had a fairly successful career in market research and at one point even considered moving to Toronto for a higher paying job offer. I was promoted 7 times in the same company and my pay rate increased by more than 30% in 7 years. I even thought of going back to school so that I could move forward in the market research.

I taught adult students before I quit to write full time. I loved teaching my students – not so thrilled about the administrative work that seemed to pile up endlessly but I still think about my students and smile. At least some of them.

But ultimately, when it came right down to it, I knew I'd never be happy unless I put my whole heart and soul into writing.

So, despite the fact that we had NO back up and that I only barely had enough client work to cover our basic living expenses – I took the jump.

Do we have some hard times? Sure. Sometimes that cheque doesn't come when it is supposed to and sometimes a project is delayed so I don't have money I thought I would. But we deal with it.

Do I have late nights? Oh ya! I'm a procrastinator so there have been more than a few nights when I've watched the sun come up as I finish a project. But I get the sleep I need eventually.

What is my point?

I quit my job to work from home full time because writing was in my heart and it was the only way I could envision myself being happy. I did it because it didn't feel right to be doing anything else. I did it because I LOVE writing.

If you have writing in your heart you will find a way to succeed.

Now, I need you to understand that I am not telling you this to brag. I'm telling you this because I want you to sit back and evaluate what you are doing.

Is writing something that you are willing to make some sacrifices for?  Is it something you miss if you don't get to do a bit of it each day?

You might also want to consider whether or not it is necessary to love what you are doing or if staying at home is just the goal.

To do:
- Make a list of your goals.  What do you really want?
- Make a list of things you like to do.  What makes you happy?
- Now make a list of ways that you could make money doing those things and be able to accomplish your goals.
- Once you have those lists, write down what you have to do to get there.
- And finally, write down the sacrifices you are willing to make

Now you have a plan!

## What You Should Consider Before Quitting Your Day Job

If you've been freelance writing or you are doing some other kind of earning activity online while still working a day job, you might be thinking of quitting. But how do you know if it is the right time? What should you think about before you take the big step?

Some of the things you should do before you put in your resignation are:

- **Do some research on the type of job you want to do from home.** Is it writing? Affiliate sales? Selling something you make? Interior design? Whatever it is you need to find out how to get your business started, how much money you can make, what tools you might need to purchase, and so on. Find people online who are successful at what they do and make contact with them. There are literally thousands of people (likely more like hundreds of thousands) who are making a living from home and most of them have an online presence. Contact them through their web page, tell them you are interested in talking with them, and ask them a few questions. Find people that are doing the kind of work you want to do and are in a similar position (single mom, main bread earner, dad with three kids and a wife, etc.). Most people are happy to talk with others that are interested in their work and many of them will be flattered you asked. Find a couple of blogs that model the kind of life that you want to lead and the kind of work that you want to do online. Take some time to really explore them. Some of the questions you might ask:

- How long have you been doing this type of work online?
- How long did it take you to move into doing it full time?
- What are your daily challenges?
- How do you manage your time?
- Where do you find support?

- **Start putting money aside.** Yes, this is a must. You can't walk into a work from home job with no money set aside to cover your behind should you have a few stumbling blocks along the way (because you will). Ok - I didn't follow my own advice when I moved into full time working from home. But I did have one major client that I had been working with for several months that would cover the most basic bills. I knew that I only needed to find a few more jobs to flesh out my income. But, it was risky. If I had any sort of emergency, like a broken tooth or a broken car, I would have had to suffer through it or find a family member that would lend me money. That's not a good place to be in so just set aside the money!

- **How much to set aside?** That depends on you and your family's needs. Figure out a budget. What do you need to get by? And do take into consideration those things that aren't necessarily "needs" but make your life livable. If you have children and you suddenly tell them that they won't be able to eat at McDonalds for the next year because mommy or daddy wants to pursue their dream they likely won't be very understanding. So cut down, but don't eliminate the things that give your family pleasure. Once you have a number that you think is fairly reasonable, multiply that by three or four. You should have at least three to four months expenses set aside.

You may not need it but you will be glad it is there!

- **Start building a client list.** Start with smaller jobs. You may have to work for less than you expected at first but these jobs can be good backup in the future. Don't undervalue yourself though! Although these clients may not pay as much, if you develop solid working relationships with them, they will always be there. Don't neglect them once you move on to bigger clients. Keep them happy. Raise your rates at a reasonable pace.

- **Start a web site with your information.** You can find some very low-cost hosting programs that are easy to use and will give you what you need. I use HostGator and have been using them for over a year and I'm very happy with them. I have several websites hosted on one account for only $9.99 a month.

- **Think about how you are going to get your name out there.** If you are Internet based, learn about promoting yourself, how and where to do it, what sites bring back good traffic, etc. Once again, talking to someone (or many someones) in your field is invaluable.

- **How are you going to handle your taxes?** Remember that once you are working from home you are going to have to deal with taxes and unless you are a bookkeeper or an accountant, you are likely going to have to have someone else deal with it for you. I was lucky. My husband was a bookkeeper and frequently handled the books for businesses. He kept up on laws and regulations for taxes and he is able to handle my taxes and make sure that I'm not getting myself into trouble! But without him, I'm sure my books would be a mess!

- **If you have children, have a plan for addressing their needs.** When you kids are little you might have to get some part time daycare in order to get work done. I know, some people do work from home with their children running around under their feet but for most people this isn't a great work environment. Teenagers can be just as distracting, believe it or not. You're going to have to set some rules and stick by them.

- **Where are you going to work?** Are you going to work from the kitchen table or will you have an office? Most people don't do well when they are working with the family running around them tossing the ball, laughing, asking questions, and more. If you need five hours to get work done you are going to have to find a place in the house that you can set up your office (if it isn't permanent) and work undisturbed. If this is not possible, you might have to find a place to work outside the home. Some people work in libraries while others work in coffee shops. You might even want to consider having an office outside of the house.

- **Do you really understand the realities of working from home full time?** If you are not sure if you have a good understanding of what the life is really like, try to find someone online that is doing similar work and has a similar situation. While the person who is single and living in different places each week may be interesting to follow and interesting to read about, they are not going to be able to give you a good picture of what you're life will be like, unless you plan to do that too, of course. If you are a single mom, try to find someone else that is a single mom, too. When you find that person, send them an email and ask them if they would be willing to answer some questions for you. They might be only able to give you time for an email but they also might be willing to chat with you over Skype for a longer period of time. You don't know until you ask. Prepare your questions ahead of time so that you don't forget what you want to ask and be respectful of the time they are offering. If they say they have 15 minutes, don't keep them busy for half an hour!

This is really only the beginning. Quitting a job isn't as easy as some think it might be because we all have different circumstances.

To Do:
- Do your research.
- Set up a plan to save money.
- Make a client list.
- Buy a domain name and hosting and set up your site.
- Find someone you can talk to that lives a life similar to yours.
- Plan for where you are going to work.

## 4 Ways to Get Online Writing Samples at the Beginning of Your Career

If you're just getting started with a freelance writing career you may have noticed that all of the good jobs ask for writing samples. But if you haven't actually had any clients yet how do you get them?

Getting writing samples online is really not that difficult. There are plenty of places that you can get your work published. But before you start with that there are a few things you should remember:

1. **Your writing samples need to have your name on it.** Without your name on it, potential clients will not know for sure that they were written by you.

2. **They need to be of good quality.** Scratch that. They need to be great quality! If you are going to use them to showcase your writing abilities, make sure that you have put the same effort into them that you would put into a clients work. Write carefully and use the 3 step writing process to ensure that they are the best you are capable of.

3. **They need to demonstrate your scope of ability.** Unless you have chosen to be a writer that focuses on a single topic (and although many writers do this eventually, I don't recommend this at the beginning; you might later fall into a specialty or find you prefer certain topics later but at the beginning you are going to need to be flexible) you will need to show potential clients that you are able to write on several different topics and that you are able to write them as if you were an expert in that field.

Now, the big question – where do you publish this writing?

**Your Own Blog**

I strongly believe that writers should spend at least some time writing for themselves. The best way to do this is with your own blog. You might want to have a niche blog if there is a specific area that you want to be able to focus on in the future. But if you haven't decided this yet you can have a blog that has several different focuses. Just separate them by categories and don't go too wide. Keep it to about 3 or 4 topics and make sure that you identify them. And remember that just because you are writing for yourself doesn't mean that others are not going to read them so spell check and edit!

## Revenue Earning Sites

When I first started writing I did a lot of work for article marketing directories. I used EzineArticles and Bukisa and I've since added InfoBarrel. There are many places where you can write articles and your name is always attached. There are some extra bonuses to writing articles for article directories. You can earn some residual income and through resource boxes and your writer's page, you can get valuable backlinks to your personal blog!

## Guest Posting

Guest posting is a great way to get some articles out there with your name on it. I won't go into great detail about guest posting because I recently blogged about it. If you missed the post, go read about why I love guest posting now.

I have several blogs that guest posts are welcome on! If you want to get some clips with your name on it check out these blogs and I'll give you full credit and backlinks to your writing site! Just click on the Contact link at the top of any of these blogs:

> *[The Social Freelance Writer](#) - accepting guest posts on blogging, social media, and freelance writing topics.*
>
> *[Live Without a Job](#) - accepting guest posts on any aspect of life without a job including types of jobs you can do (you should actually be earning a living from what you write about though), organization, saving money, and more.*

You can also find places to guest post by doing a Google search for things like, "guest posts careers" or whatever you topic of specialty is.

And of course, there are sites where you can specifically hook up with people that are looking for guest post. Some of the sites worth exploring are:

> *[My Blog Guest](#) - submit posts to be used as guest posts.*
>
> *[Blogger Linkup](#) - find places that are looking for guest posts.*
>
> *[Triberr](#) - if you are in a tribe already you can go to the Bonfires section and find people that are looking for guest posts.*

**Volunteer Work**

Finally, you can think a little less traditionally, too. Don't be afraid to be creative about getting your name out there on articles. If you have an organization that you are particularly fond of, volunteer to write something for them. Do you have a friend that needs help on their site? Offer to help them out. Look for opportunities to get published samples online.

And once you have them? Be picky! Don't give every potential client the same list of published samples. Choose samples that are most closely related to what they are looking for. If they are looking for something in the health care niche – find an article that is related. Or if they want how-to articles make sure that you choose one of your samples that are written in that style.

Getting samples is not hard – making sure that you have samples that reflect your abilities is more challenging.

To Do:
**Write 5 great blog posts or articles. Make them fabulous with 600-1000 words each. Use the above suggestions to find homes for them.**

## Create a Professional Writer Site to Direct People To!

Your professional freelance writer site is your home base. You can have a blog with it or you can set it up as a stand-alone site. It must be professional and it must be well put together if you want people to hire you!

So, first - what platform are you going to use?

I have a strong preference for WordPress with your own hosting for the simple fact that it is professional looking and there are many ways that you can adapt it to suit your needs. But it is by all means not the only place where you can set up your home. However, please get your own domain and set it up on the place where you host your site. Don't buy your domain from the place where your site will be hosted. Why? I'm of the firm belief that you should never give control to any one place. Also, having it set up somewhere for free tells others that you don't take your business seriously. And you do, don't you?

Choose a domain that is either your full name or your business name - nothing cutesy!

That being said here are a few places you might consider setting up your professional site:

Webs.com

Yola.com

Blogger.com

WordPress.com

All of these sites will allow you to purchase a domain and they will handle the hosting but once again, I believe you should keep the two separate. I use Namecheap for buying all of my domains and they have never steered me wrong.

You'll need to choose a simple design that isn't too fancy. You can add some of your own flavor to it but don't go overboard.

Now, you need to put content on your site that will give clients the feeling that you are right for the job!

Pages you should include:

*Home Page:* Tell the client why they should hire you!

*About Me:* Tell people who you are; remember though, that they don't want to know what your hobbies are (unless it pertains to your specialty) but they do want to know why you are the best person for the job. This is like a sales page and **you** are what you are selling.

*Resume and/or Sample*: Some people don't like to put a resume on their site but I think a resume is important.  You don't have to include details about where you live or anything that can put your identity at risk but you should include your skills, sites you currently write for, and experiences you have had that relate to the kind of writing you do.  You should at the very least include samples with links.

*Services:* This is pretty basic.  What services do offer?  Blog writing, article writing, white pages, reports, ebooks - include everything that you are able to offer the client.

*Testimonials:*  Of course, if you don't have testimonials, don't include this page but once you have had a couple jobs you can ask clients if you can include a comment from them.  Some writers send out comment forms when they complete a gig.  If you do this, when you get a good comment from a client ask them if you can use it.

*Contact:* Clients need to have a way to contact you.  Either use a contact form (most sites make these available) or at the very least and email address.  Some like to include their Skype name, as well.

*Blog:* You might want to have a blog connected to your site.  If you do, keep in mind this is a blog for clients, not for other writers.  Clients don't care what writing challenges you are coming across or how much more money you need to make this month.  Posts like this may actually discourage clients from hiring you. Write useful blog posts that can help clients and always direct them back to your main page.

Above all, make sure that you have no spelling mistakes and use good writing.  Pretend that you are putting it together for a potential client because really, your professional site is going to be your first sample!

To Do:
- **Choose a domain name.**
- **Find a place to host your site.**
- **Set up pages on your site.**
- **Proofread each page scrupulously!**

## 20 Ways to Promote Your Professional Freelance Writer Site

One thing writers hear often is that they need to have a professional site (or a portfolio site) if they want to get private clients. And I completely agree.

Your professional site is like your office online. It is the place where you can direct clients when they want to find you. It is the place where you can hand out promo material (a free ebook, a free report, etc.) and sell your skills.

But how do you promote it once it is up and ready?

Here are ideas for promoting your professional freelance writer site:

1.     **Put it in your email signature.** Almost every email provider gives you an option to set up a signature. Think about all those jokes and stuff that you forward to your friends. How many times to they get forwarded to other people? If you don't forward things too often you could end up having your email signature forwarded to many people.

2. **Put it in the signature of any forums you are on.** I click on signature links all the time if they are well written. You don't have to just put the name of your site as a link. You can include a line that makes it more appealing and tells people what your site is about. Many forum links allow up to 3 lines so take advantage of them!

3. **Create a Squidoo "About Me" page.** This can be a fun and entertaining way to introduce yourself to people and to explain what you do. Remember to keep the focus on what the benefit is for them and not on you.

4. **Create an [About.me](About.me) page.** This is one of my favorite ways of getting backlinks to a site and of making a great sales pitch. If you have an elevator pitch, this is the place to use it. You can include different kinds of links, too - your web site, your Twitter, your Facebook, or any other way that you want to connect with people.

5. **Create a [MyOnePage](MyOnePage) business card.** This is basically just what it sounds like - a business card with links to your sites, your email address, and other ways of connecting with people. I actually get several emails a month directly from this site from people that are interested in my services. Others go right to my professional freelance writer site and then contact me from there.

6.   **Make an "About Me" page on HubPages.** Just like with the Squidoo page you have a lot of room to be creative but make sure that your focus is on the reader and what you can do for them.

7.   **Put together a <u>completed LinkedIn page</u>.** LinkedIn gets some great search engine results and there is a place to link to your site. Take this opportunity to sell the reader on what you can offer them and how you can bring them benefits.

8.   **Write articles about your specialty or about why people should hire a blogger/press release writer/ghostwriter/etc. and post them on article marketing sites with *proper anchors*.** Anchors are the terms that you use to create your link and they tell search engines what your site is about. You should choose words that people actually search for so make sure that you do a little bit of keyword research. Try to find a term that is not overly saturated. For example, don't just use the term "writer" as your link. Instead use something more descriptive like "career blog writer" or "medical profession writer". These terms are less likely to be targeted by as many writers and if you are consistent you are more likely to get to the top of the search engines results when people search for these terms.

Keep in mind that Google has made some major changes in their algorithms in the past year. One of those changes includes the Panda updates and part of that had to do with anchors for links. If you always use the same one or two anchors, Google will assume you are over-working the system and you will likely get penalized. Use a variety of anchors for your keywords and once in awhile throw in a plain hyperlink (like http://daniellemcgaw.com) or link your site to "click here" or "read more". That will decrease your chances of getting penalized by Google.

9. **Make a site tour video and put it on YouTube**. YouTube can be an excellent source of traffic if you remember to use tags in your video when you post it. Also use the keyword terms that you looked up in the previous point as tags for your video. Use them not only in your tags but also in the description and in the title. When you put together your description put your full url at the beginning, including the http:// part. This will make your link clickable and it will ensure that if you video is embedded on someone else's site the link will be there when they embed it if the description is included (as it often is!).

10. **Turn those articles you wrote into videos and put them on YouTube.** People go to YouTube for information so all those articles that

you wrote can do double time by being recorded in an audio file. You can use pictures to go alone with your audio or you can create a PowerPoint or a Prezi presentation and record it using software like Screencast-o-matic (there's a free version and a paid version). This is my favorite software for doing screencasts.

11. **Create a static Blogger blog with re-written articles from those you put on the article marketing sites.** Make it informative and create links in each blog post to different pages on your web sites. Don't forget to use good anchor text!

12. **Create a static WordPress.com blog with re-written articles from those you put on the article marketing sites.** Same as above!

13. **Make audio recordings of the articles that you have written and put them on sites like audioboo.com.** This is a free site that allows you to create audio that you can share. You can embed them on other sites, too. Audioboo now allows you to put your audio on iTunes as a podcast, which can give you even more exposure!

14. **Social bookmark them (Digg, Delicious, etc.)!** I use two sites to do social bookmarking in bulk. There are many great sites for social bookmarking but choose a few that you like and

use them consistently. You can bookmark the articles you wrote for point #8 and the YouTube videos you made and the Blogger and WordPress blogs you made, too!

15. **Tweet it.** Twitter can be a great source of traffic if you have a lot of followers. And don't just tweet it once. Tweet it periodically at different times so that you will reach different groups of people. And remember that short tweets followed by "please RT" or "please re-tweet" get re-tweeted by others more often!

16. **Announce it on your Facebook page.** And remember that Facebook lets you leave an url to your site in your About Me section so leave it there, too!

17. **Put the articles you've written on Scribd.com.** Make sure that you put your url in the footer of the document. This can be a great place to get some extra traffic. You can put the articles up one by one or you can create a couple of well put together articles by combining several of them into one article.

18. **Answer relevant questions on Yahoo Answers.** After you have answered a certain number of questions you can start leaving live links!

19. **Send an email to past clients to let them know your site is active and ask them to forward the link to anyone that they think could benefit from your services.** If your clients were happy with your services they will be more than happy to recommend you when the opportunity arises.

20. **Put it on a business card; use the business card!!!** There are so many places you can use business cards. Leave them in library books, leave them on the counter at the bank after you fill in your deposit slip, keep them handy to pass out when someone asks what you do - think creatively and you will likely find many uses for your business cards.

To Do:
Pick one of these things to do each week. Or even every day! Just make a point to start promoting your site. Add these things into your work plan each day and you will find that you will start seeing results!

## How Dare You Write for Peanuts?

You know, I have to say that I am just getting so tired of this debate. Some writers think that they have the right to judge those who write for low pay. Some writers think that because they are making "more" (whatever that may be to them) that other writers should turn away low paying writing gigs because they are worth more.

Well, they may or may not be worth "more" but really, who are you to say what pay they should write for?

Someone posted about this on a writer's forum I frequent. I generally do not get involved in these things but I'm so sick of hearing it. The general gist of the original post was that writers shouldn't be writing for less than 2 cents/word and that if they couldn't get work for that much they would be better off putting the work on their own blog and putting up Google Adsense and making money from that.

My reply:

*Honestly, I am just sick to death of hearing this debate.*

*There are different markets out there for everything so why shouldn't writing be the same? The markets that one cent a word writers are writing for is completely different from the five cent a word markets. The writers are different, too, with different needs.*

*Remember for some writers $10 an hour is more than they have ever made at a regular job. So, to them, one cent a word is great when you can pound out 4 500 word articles in an hour because they are just that easy. I started out writing at 1 cent a word and I still occasionally take writing at that rate if it is super simple and requires very little thinking. I do re-writing at that rate because I can do a 500 word article re-write in about 8 minutes.*

*You can tell me what I "should" be writing for all you want but the bottom line is that I am going to do whatever I need to do to support my family. I am going to do whatever I need to do to NOT have to leave the house to go to a job so that I can be here for my kids and for my often sick husband. And NO ONE has the right to tell me that I should stop writing for low rates when I need to.*

*You know, the money I am making now is substantially higher than it was at any of the outside the house jobs I've ever had but I'd bet that there are lots of you who would think, "That's all she makes?" But you know, when my daughter was a baby I was working my butt off at minimum wage as a cook – working stupid hours and sweating in a hot kitchen. And I make a hell of a lot more than that now. 3 years ago I was working in a market research company and still making less than $20 an hour, plus I had to pay for transportation and buy nice clothes and other expenses that go with working in an office.*

*So, if a woman (or man for that matter) decides to take low paying jobs (whether writing or anything else) in order to make her family a priority it is no one's business but her own.*

*There is NOTHING wrong with taking a lower pay to take care of the one's you love and to be with them.*

And I didn't think to put this part but regarding putting content on your own blog and putting up ads – well, you need traffic to get money from ads don't you.  And it is just not that simple.  You know, I've had this blog up for over a year and I don't think I've made a cent from it.  And my traffic, quite frankly, sucks.  I'm just not a great marketer.  I know that.  But I love this blog, so I keep working at it.  Will it be profitable someday?  I hope so.  Is it now?  Not really.

To me, the bottom line is that you do what you need to do and what you are comfortable with.  If you're comfortable writing for peanuts, you enjoy it, and it is accomplishing whatever the purpose is then keep doing what you are doing.  But if you want to make more money?  There are ways and those who want to will find them.

Write for peanuts if you want to – but if you don't want to, work hard, read from the experts, and apply for bigger jobs – they will come!

**Added:

Now, when I wrote this I was pretty excited.  I was good and worked up because I really hate it when other writers (or anyone for that matter) try to tell me that I shouldn't work at a rate.  It is my choice.  Sometimes I have bills to pay or there's an emergency and I'd do damn near anything to get that extra money in my PayPal account.

But I want you to understand that you don't HAVE to work for peanuts if you don't want to. There are some very good paying gigs out there and if you have skill and learn to market yourself, you could get those gigs if you want to. It takes time but put the work into it and understand that if you are getting paid $1 a word you're going to have to put more time into it. You're going to have to do more than just a bit of online research and you're going to have to THINK. You will need to be able to produce content that is not being put out there by other sites online. It does take work.

Personally, I prefer not to have to think too much, so sometimes I do take lower paying gigs. I have one semi-ongoing gig where I write a short synopsis of movies and insert a couple of keywords. Each one takes about 3 minutes to write at most. I can't complain about it and when I don't have the energy to think too much it fits the bill.

Do what works for you and don't let anyone tell you that you are doing it wrong.

To Do:
**Experiment with different pay levels when working with private clients. What level of pay can you work at comfortably without getting stressed out? What level of pay makes you happiest?**

## 50 Reasons Freelance Writers Should Be Using Social Media

When it comes right down to it, I know that as a freelance writer, you are busy. Whether you are a freelance writer that supplements the household income by writing or a freelance writer that is working part-time or a freelance writer that using writing as the main source of income for the household, we all have to make sure that our time is efficient.

And it is true – social media can be a big time sucker if you aren't using it with purpose. But have a focus, and know why you're using it and social media can be a great investment of your time.

Why? Well, there are 50 good reasons why!

**Here are 50 reasons why you should be using social media:**

# To Build Awareness

1. **Promote your website.** Your website has no value whatsoever if no one knows about it. Whether you have a blog or a simple site that displays the services you offer and

some samples, you need to be found for it to have value.

2. **Establish a web presence.** Potential clients will Google you and if they find nothing they will assume that you are new and inexperienced.

3. **Promote your articles.** Whether you are writing articles for back links or for residual income, they are worthless if no one is reading them.

4. **Build a brand.** Who do people buy from? Usually, they buy from brands they are familiar with. So, whether you are using a business name or your given name as your brand, increase awareness of it.

5. **Give away free reports**. Free reports can show off your skill as a writer and your knowledge of a specific niche. You can also give potential clients a prime example of a product that they also can use to promote their business. Give people the permission to share your free reports.

6. **Demonstrate your strong ethics.** By being professional, respectful, and mature you can display a major characteristic that clients look for.

7. **Share your resume.** There are several ways that you can share your resume such as a page on your site, your LinkedIn profile, or one of the many resume building websites that are available.

8. **Let people attach a face to your brand.** People feel closer when there is a face that they can identify. They like to know that there is someone behind the brand and they are more likely to feel they can trust you.

9. **Share what others say about you.** When others have good things to say it validates what you have been saying all along. People are much more likely to believe what someone says about you than what you say about you.

10. **Stay in the forefront of people's minds.** When people have writing work you don't want them to think, "How am I going to find a writer?" You want them to think of you because they already know you are a writer and they believe that they can trust you.

## To Learn

1. **Become an expert in your niche.** If you write about a specific topic, you need to make sure that you present yourself as an expert.

2. **Find concise batches of information through lists.** Most social media sites have some sort of list function. Use it.

3. **Find people to interview.** Our articles are more valuable when they have real people in them. Also, interviews with professionals give your work credibility.

4. **Find out about industry events.** Industry events give you the chance to network on a whole new level. Learn, make new friends, and find business opportunities.

5. **Find off-line promotional opportunities.** Speak at an event, offer a free copy of a book, or give someone a quote to use.

6. **Find out about free webinars.** You'll learn loads and you can often save the audio version to refer back to later.

7. **Learn more about SEO** – if you're a writer this is not negotiable.

8. **Find new slants to articles you've already written.** Those articles that took you half an hour to write can be re-worked for a different market and pay again.

9. **Ask questions.** There are so many people out there that are willing to share what they know – all you have to do is ask!

10. **Get recommendations and share them.** You can get recommendations for products, service, tools, and more. Don't rely on advertising. Experience is a much better means of evaluating the value of a product or service.

11. **Learn new skills.** New skills will only make your business stronger. The more value you can offer clients the more you can charge.

12. **Beat writer's block.** We all get it from time to time. Social media offers multitudes of opportunities to get past it.

13. **Find tools to make your business easier.** Finding the right tools to run your business can make a difference between working 4 hours a day or 6 hours a day.

14. **Find resources for support.** Knowing where to go to get help or where you can find other supports as a writer can ensure that

this stays a career you love and not a job that needs to get done.

15. **Be more efficient** by using tools that allow you to use more than one social media source at once (you all know I love Hootsuite!).

16. **Increase your writing skills.** Writing for social media content involves being very concise. It's good practice to communicate with fewer words.

17. **Create a swipe file.** Ever find yourself running out of ideas to write about when you write in the same niche (even if it is just for a period of time)? A swipe file can make your job a lot easier and the ideas you get from social media can help you create your own.

18. **Get motivation.** Let's face it – we all need a little motivation from time to time. Social media networks are filled with people and ideas that can motivate you.

19. **Be more portable.** Your work and the people you work with can follow you around.

20. **Get information.** How do you flesh out those articles? How do you grow as a writer?

How do you develop new skills? All by finding and putting to use information.

## To Build Relationships

1. **Find a mentor.** Gee, I can't tell you how much having a mentor has helped me. If it were not for the fact that [Sharon Hurley Hall](#) believed in me, I don't know if I would have pursued freelance writing as a career.

2. **Mentor others.** Do you have experience and knowledge? I'm sure you do. Give back to the community by sharing what you know with someone new.

3. **Find places to guest post.** Guest posting can be a great way to enter a new clique.

4. **Find other writers/business people to collaborate with.** Joint projects can help you expand your circle and increase your chances of meeting new potential clients and partners.

5. **Arrange real life meetings.** Whether it is clients, partners, or just other writer friends, real life meetings just make what you start online stronger.

6. **Find places to outsource things you don't like to do or aren't good at.** No one can be

great at everything and finding the people who can do certain tasks better can save you time and money.

7. **Connect your networks.** You are likely on more than one network so make sure that people can find you where ever they go.

8. **Get peer feedback.** Others often see things differently than you do. Ask for their opinions so that you can see it, too.

9. **Develop relationships with other writers.** We all need friends that understand us – other writers!

## To Increase Income

1. **Increase residual income possibilities.** Are your writing articles on residual earning sites or maybe trying to sell an eBook or trying to make money from advertising on your blog? Have a social media presence increases your exposure.

2. **Find jobs.** Yes, you can find jobs. There are many ways to do this in social media and some sites (like LinkedIn) are better than others but there are other opportunities as well.

3. **Develop relationship with potential clients.** People use the services and products of their "friends" – so be friendly!

4. **Find out where your clients are hanging out.** Why be where they aren't?

5. **Find out what clients really need!** No one will use your services if they don't really need them.

6. **Pitch ideas to potential clients.** Feel them out and throw out an idea or two.

7. **Expand your market.** If you normally provide your writing services for online content companies you might be able to expand to individuals or larger bricks and mortar companies.

8. **Launch your own product.** With your own products you keep all the income.

9. **Understand your clients.** Find out what they think, what they value, what kind of education they have. The more information you have about them the more likely you are to be able to market yourself to them.

10. **Get more exposure to a wider array of clients.** When you are active on social media sites people start to know you as "the writer" and when they have a need for someone that offers your service they are more likely to come to you. Also, if you connect with people and develop relationships with them, they will be more likely to

recommend you if someone they know is looking for a writer.

11. **Build your email list.** Don't have an email list?  Start building one then!  When someone joins an email list it is an open invitation for you to send them information and special offers!

To Do:
- Create a Twitter account, a Facebook Profile, and a Facebook Page if you do not already have these.
- Outline a plan for using each of these accounts on a daily basis and have a goal each day.
- Track what you are doing and the results you are getting.
- Analyze your progress over time.

## Freelance Writers Can Stay Motivated with These 7 Tips

Staying motivated is one of the things that I think everyone has a hard time with at one point or another. Sometimes we get frustrated with a project because it is not going the way we think it should. Other times we lose motivation because we get tired of doing the same thing day after day. When everything seems to be the same day after day motivation is often the first thing to go out the door. But if we want the money to keep coming in we need to find ways to get fired up about what we are doing so that we can continue.

Here are some of the ways that I stay motivated (and trust me, since I've started working at home full-time I've had to use a few of these!):

1. **Read success stories.** Sometimes when you feel like you are just spinning your wheels reading the successes of others can help you get going again. I find it especially helpful when I realize that other successful

writers and online entrepreneurs have often gone through the same things as I do.

You can find success stories on blogs in the form of About pages or interviews but you can find them in other places as well. If you write for residual earnings you might find some great stories on forums. Try googling "freelance writing success story" or "freelance writer interview" and other similar phrases and you will likely find some great inspiration!

2. **Write down your successes.** You haven't gotten to where you are without successes. You started from nowhere and now you're...where are you? Write down the things that you have succeeded at, the things you have taught yourself, and the challenges you have overcome to get where you are.

3. **Remember that this is your job.** Sometimes you have to remind yourself that doctors don't get paid when they are not in the mood to operate and you won't get paid if you are not in the mood to write. If you want to pay the bills and eat and have money to go out and do fun things you need to write. Some days are going to be

more exciting than others but you still need to get down to business.

4. **Reward yourself.** Sometimes we need something a little bit extra to get the work done so give yourself rewards when you have completed a task. It could be a trip to the coffee shop, a massage, or even just an hour to sit still and read a book that you like.

5. **Get a writing buddy.** When you need a lift up you can turn to each other. Find someone with an upbeat attitude. Don't forget to be their cheer captain sometimes, too, though. Make a set time to contact each other either daily or weekly. Share your successes and challenges. You might even get a group together and chat on Skype or in a Google Hangout a couple times a week. Heck, you can even write together all day long if you want and take assigned breaks to stop and chat. Who needs a water cooler? You have the whole online world at your fingertips!

6. **Put the editor aside.** When you are writing, just write. Don't let the editor come in and tell you how much you suck. Don't let the editor stifle your creativity. Let the editor

come out only when you are done writing. Then they can do their job.

7. **Find the ultimate inspiration.** What have you always wanted to do with your writing? Write a book? Then design a cover for the book and put in on your bulletin board. Do you want to publish an article in the New Yorker? Then keep a copy on your desk where you can see it. Or maybe you've always wanted to go to Paris. Put a beautiful Paris print on the wall.

We all need a little motivation to keep going at times so find out what kinds of things will motivate you. Remember that no one gets promoted to the vice-president over night – you need to work your way up and you'll need motivation to keep climbing that ladder.

To Do:
- Create a list of your successes to refer back to when you need the motivation
- Find a writing buddy or a group of writing buddies. Commit to supporting one another.
- Find your ultimate inspiration and find something physical to represent it and put it where you can see it while you work.

## 9 Ways for Freelance Writers to Improve Their Proofreading Skills

Some people think that you are either good at proofreading or you aren't. The fact of the matter is that proofreading is a skill that requires practice. Even if you are not great at proofreading now you can use some of these tips to improve your proofreading skills and become an even better freelancer. Here are some ways to become a better proofreader:

1. **Don't just focus on misspelled words.** You should watch for them because they are not all going to be caught by the spell checker, but you need to watch for other things as well. Watch for repetitious words, readability, and incorrect sentence structure.

2. **Set the document aside for awhile.** When you give the article some time you can return with fresh eyes and you will be more likely to catch your mistakes. Finish writing, take a break, and then come back to it.

3. **Read what is actually on the page.** Sometimes your mind makes you think that

you are reading what you want to read but there are actually mistakes. You need to focus on the words that are on the page instead of the words you meant to write.

4. **Watch for common mistakes.** You know what mistakes you make most often. I know one that I have to watch for is serial commas. In Canada it is the accepted way to use commas (milk, bread, and butter) but since most of my clients are American I have to make sure that there are not serial commas in my text (milk, bread and butter).

5. **Slowly read out loud.** If you read your article out loud you can often "hear" your mistakes. You can hear when the sentence just sounds weird. If you have repeated a word several times you will hear the repetition.

6. **Work with a partner.** If you can it is a great idea to work with someone. Send your articles back and forth and proofread them for each other. My husband and I are both writers and we often proofread each other's work. When I'm especially tired and have been writing a lot, having my husband proofread my work before I send it in is very helpful.

7. **Watch for words that are wrong and right at the same time.** Words like to and too are both spelled right but they have different situations where they are correct. See and sea are both spelled correctly but they can be incorrect if they are used in the wrong context.

8. **Keep your guard up.** When you let your guard down and are not paying attention, that is when you will start making mistakes.

9. **Don't settle for a quick glance at your article.** Read it over several times and make sure you give it the attention it deserves.

To Do:
Create a checklist to use when you are proofreading. It could look something like this:

- I've read it out loud
- I've read it in my head
- I've had someone else read it
- I've let it sit for a day
- I've read it through one more time

Of course, you can make this as specific as you like and integrate particular problems you may have.

## **Get Into the Writing Zone: Environment**

Do you find that you are having a hard time getting into the writer's zone? You know what I mean – that place where everything just goes smoothly. The words flow, the ideas come fast and furious, and you aren't getting distracted. It happens to every writer at some point or another.

Maybe it is your environment.

Your environment can have a strong effect on how well you are able to do your work. It can make the difference between a day where things get done and a day where you've felt busy but look back and realize that you have really accomplished very little.

Environment covers a lot of areas:

- **Family:** When your family is constantly at your side it can be difficult to focus on writing. It seems like no matter what age kids are they need you. Younger children need you to attend to their basic needs and kids of all ages need you to attend to their emotional needs. I know that my teen children go batty if they don't see me in the house. They need to tell me a joke or have me brush their hair (even though they've been brushing their own hair for 10 years now!). Timing is going to be critical here and you might have to work after they have gone to bed or before they get up or while they are in school.

Try to set up working hours when you are absolutely not to be bothered. If your kids are in school that is obviously going to be a more productive time for you so try to get as much work done then as possible. If your children are young you might have to enlist in the help of your partner. Hopefully they are supportive of your work and will be on board when you tell them that they need to be in charge during certain hours. That means that they will need to actively be with the children and not just hanging out in the house.

- **Noise:** Some people need dead quiet to focus while others need some background noise. I know that when I was working as a receptionist I needed the radio on to help me block out the noise of other staff members. Everyone seemed to think that my desk was a great place to congregate and talk about the weekend but if I had the radio on it seemed to distract me from their noise. Find out what works best for you.

Here are a couple great sites for background noise that isn't music:

- ❖ Do Nothing for Two Minutes: The point of this site is to do nothing and relax but even after the 2 minute timer runs out the sound track continues.
- ❖ Rainy Mood: Who doesn't love the sound of rain? This is just enough to cover outside noise but not distracting at all. I could listen to this all day long!
- ❖ Nature Sounds For Me: Create your own sound track with your favorite sounds. The beach? Fire? The purr of a cat? You got it! You can decide what sound comes across the loudest and what combination of sounds you want. You can save it as a link or even download it to put on an MP3 player.
- ❖ Mood Turn: This one gives you a selection of sounds to choose from - the beach, the forest, birds, dolphins or others.

- **Clothes**:  Get comfortable.  If you're not comfortable you're going to be restless and you won't be able to focus on working.

- **Your desk:** Assuming you have a desk, you should try to keep it clear and uncluttered. I know that some people think that a messy desk is just the sign of a busy person (I used to be one of those people) but if you only have the things you need at hand (a notebook for notes, a pen, your computer) in front of you, you are less likely to get distracted by the note that you haven't signed for your kid's school yet or the grocery list that you need to make later.

   I find it helpful to keep as many things on my computer as possible.  Not only does that make my business more portable but it also keeps fewer things ON my desk!  It is much easier to close a window than it is to have to hide something on your desk if it is distracting you.

- **Lighting:** Dull lighting can make you feel drowsy but lighting that is too bright can give you a headache.  Make sure that the lighting in your work space is adequate but not so bright that it will throw off your concentration.

What are some of the other environmental factors that might cause you to lose concentration?

To Do:

Try to set up a place and time where you will work most of the time. You don't have to have an office but you do have to have an environment that will allow you to focus on your work.

Experiment with sound, lighting, and hours to see what works best for you. Keep track of the changes you make over a two week period so you can see how each change affects your work efficiency.

## How to Avoid Getting Scammed When Applying For Writing Gigs

As writers we are always wary of getting scammed by people that are trying to take advantage of us. We hear about it all the time and it has happened to many of us. It hasn't happened to me yet so I don't know if I'm just lucky or if I'm just good at picking out the bad ones.

Knowing that there are scammers out there shouldn't stop you from applying for jobs. You do need to watch for the red flags though, and those little flags can prevent you from doing a lot of work that you won't get paid for.

### *"Send Me an Article on This Topic"*

Watch out for people who want you to do the first article on spec or they want you to do the first one for free. This is how they get their content for their sites and they likely are not actually paying many, if any, writers for actual work. Why should they when naïve writers will send off their hard work with a hope and a prayer?

You should expect to provide samples, but work that you have already written should give them enough information to tell them what kind of work that you are capable of.  Have samples online at places like Bukisa or Associated Content that you can direct potential clients to.  Make sure your samples are good!

On occasion I have a potential client that needs work in a very specific niche and they want a sample from that field.  If they ask for a sample for a topic that I don't have, I'll write the sample, put it up at InfoBarrel or HubPages, and then send them the link to it.  That way, I know that it isn't going to get stolen and they get proof that I'm capable of writing for that specific niche.

Note that test articles are not always the same as free article requests.  Many companies will ask for a test article or even several to see if you can follow through with their directions.  For some companies, this is an important part of the hiring process and I completely understand it.  Verify that you will get paid for the test articles before completing them.

> *"Up to $100 for 500 words - no research needed!"*

Now before you get excited, I will admit that there are companies out there that do pay $100 for 500 words but I'm pretty sure that the work is not easy. If they claim that the work is easy and that it will only take you small amount of time to do it but say they are paying a lot more than you know it is worth, look around for other red flags.

Sometimes they use this as a lure to get writers to write for low fees first, and promise that if they are good the real money will come. It rarely does but by the time the writers figure it out they have already gotten loads of content from them and there are other naïve writers waiting to make their millions.

There is one company in particular that uses this as a lure to writers. When you apply you will be directed to a web site where you need to sign up to get access to all these great high paying gigs. What you are signing up for is a trial membership. Once you have finished your trial you will be asked to pay to have access to the writing gig. Unfortunately, most of the gigs are low paying and it takes a lot of time to sift through them to find decent paying gigs. And even if you don't stay on, you'll continue to get annoying emails from them for a long time! Stay away from them! I'd give you a name but they are constantly changing names because there are so many complaints about them. Just don't sign up for sites like this and you should be safe.

> *"For a small fee you get access to millions of unseen jobs!"*

First, you should never have to pay to get work. Does a doctor pay to get a listing of sick patients? Does a mechanic pay to find out who needs their car fixed? Of course not. People come to you or you apply for jobs but you don't pay out money to get jobs.

Many places write an ad that looks like a job and then they direct you to a site where they encourage you to sign up for the first week for free and only "this much" after that (just like the one I mentioned above). They act like they are service providers because they know damn well that they can't promise you work. In fact, even if you do pay the "small monthly fee" you still have to apply for the jobs and compete with all the other people that are paying to get access to the jobs.

> *"Great opportunity for stay at home moms and students!"*

A lot of people think that moms who work from home and students will work for anything and will do anything. Beware of people who single out these groups. They may be expecting a lot of work for very little compensation.

Sometimes it is really hard to tell but you think it is worth checking out. If this is the case, read the email that you get in reply very carefully. They should give details about who they are, their websites, the name of their company, and other information that will identify them. If they don't give that information, ask for it – the scammers will try to dance their way around your questions.

Keep applying for jobs but be smart. Watch for those little warning signs and if your gut is telling you to back out there is likely a good reason. Follow your instincts.

**To Do:**
**Create a checklist of red flags to watch for when applying for jobs. Print it out and keep it near your work area so that you can see it and use it to decide what jobs to apply for.**

## Where to Find Writing Gigs

You didn't think I was going to finish off this book without pointing you in the right direction for finding clients did you? Of course not!

There are two basic kinds of writing gigs. One is content mills and the other is private clients. There are advantages and disadvantages of each one. Personally, I prefer private clients because I feel that it gives me more say about what kind of topics I write about.

## Content Mills

Since I'm not a big content mill person I'm not even going to try to put together a massive list. But I am going to tell you where to find it.

[This thread](#) at the WAHM forum is filled with places that are looking for writers. Personally, I'd start from the last post and work my way backwards because some of the ones at the beginning might not be hiring anymore or they might not even be active.

My friend Janis also has [pretty massive list of sites that hire writers](#).

And finally - one of the most comprehensive sites that hire writers is here. I do like this one because you can order it by pay or by country or whatever. It is pretty useful.

## Private Clients

Now, if you really want to get private clients you are going to have to put some work into it. That means applying for jobs, making cold calls/cold emails, and a whole lot of thinking outside the box.

These are the sites that I visit regularly when I need to get some more work:

**Facebook4Freelancers.com : Freelance Writing Jobs : Freelancing Group**

**Jobs for Bloggers - ProBlogger Job Board**

**Freelance Job Openings : Hire a Freelancer!**

**Blogging Pro Job Board**

**Write Jobs**

**Freelance Writing Jobs**

## CraigsList

Those are just a few of the places I look because they often have good jobs. Apply to everything you think looks good. Don't judge on the legitimacy of the job until you have the chance to talk to a real person via email or chat. Then, use that red flag check list you made to decide on whether it is worth pursuing.

Of course, if you really want good private clients, don't stop there.

What do I mean? I mean, you need to get out there and start making connections. Yes, more social media.

The last bunch of jobs I have gotten have all been a direct result of my social media efforts. One client is a super big passive income guy that has a podcast and a very famous site. He also has niches sites and I've written an ebook for him and now blog posts. And he pays very nicely. I made contact with him through Facebook and got the job because of my Facebook networking.

A couple other jobs have come from Twitter. I get on there and talk to people, I talk about my writing, and I let people get to know me. Several people have come to me because they knew I was "the writer".

Don't sit around and wait for private clients to come to you (even though your site is pretty kick ass by now I hope!). Make yourself available and go to them!

## Resources

# Blogs worth reading:

- ❖ Freelance Writing: Achieve Freelance Writing Success
- ❖ Get Paid to Write Online
- ❖ Make a Living Writing
- ❖ Productive Writers: Work Less, Earn More, Live More
- ❖ Quips and Tips for Successful Writers
- ❖ Brandi-Ann Uyemura: Not just a writer but a creative connoisseur…

# Setting Up Your Site:

- ❖ Get a domain at NameCheap.com
- ❖ Find web site hosting at Blue Host or HostGator
- ❖ Or use Yola.com
- ❖ Or use Webs.com
- ❖ Or use Blogger.com
- ❖ Or use WordPress.com

## Promoting Your Site

- About.me
- OnePage
- LinkedIn
- Twitter
- Facebook
- YouTube
- Vimeo
- Blogger
- WordPress
- Audioboo
- Cinchcast
- IMAutomator
- OnlyWire
- Scribd
- Squidoo
- HubPages
- InfoBarrel
- Other article marketing sites

## Calming Background Noise:

- Do Nothing for Two Minutes
- Rainy Mood
- Nature Sounds For Me
- Mood Turn

## Sites for guest posting:

- *The Social Freelance Writer*

- [Live Without a Job](#)
- [Anxiety and Panic Headquarters](#)
- [How to be a Freelance Writer](#)
- [My Blog Guest](#)
- [Blogger Linkup](#)

P.S. I've been working on this compilation of posts and trying to improve it for awhile now. If there are mistakes please forgive me! LOL

www.ingramcontent.com/pod-product-compliance
Lightning Source LLC
Chambersburg PA
CBHW071808170526
45167CB00003B/1224